Book of Prayers

Berkeley Hills Books
Titles by M. K. Gandhi

Book of Prayers
Prayer
Vows and Observances
The Way to God

Book of Prayers

MOHANDAS K. GANDHI

Edited by John Strohmeier
Foreword by Arun Gandhi
Introduction by Michael N. Nagler

Berkeley Hills Books
Berkeley, California

Published by
Berkeley Hills Books
P. O. Box 9877
Berkeley, California 94709
www.berkeleyhills.com

Cover design by Elysium, San Francisco.
Cover Photo © CORBIS/Bettman.
Manufactured in the United States of America.
Distributed by Publishers Group West.

3   5   7   9   10   8   6   4   2

Library of Congress Cataloging-in-Publication Data

Ashram Bhajanavali. English.
    Book of Prayers / translated into English by Mohandas K. Gandhi ;
foreword by Arun Gandhi ; introduction by Michael N. Nagler ; edited
by John Strohmeier.
    p.   cm.
    Selection of prayers from Gujarati.
    ISBN 1-893163-02-4 (pa. alk. paper)
    1. Hinduism--Prayer books and devotions--English. 2. Islam-
-Prayer books and devotions--English.   I. Gandhi, Mahatma,
1869-1948. II. Strohmeier, John. Title.
BL 1236.22.A84   1999
294.5'433--dc21   99-20643
                                                        CIP

Contents

Publisher's Note

This selection of prayers was made from Mahatma Gandhi's English translation of *Ashram Bhajanavali*, the prayer book and hymnal of Satyagraha Ashram. The translation was completed between May and December 1930, and published in 1971 by the Government of India in *The Collected Works of Mahatma Gandhi* (vol. XLIV, pp. 386-465).

Minimal changes were made to the original text for the present edition. The prose format of each passage was divided into verses; slight alterations in wording were made to one line of the first prayer and four lines elsewhere; and spelling, capitalization and punctuation were edited to conform to contemporary American usage. Notes appended to several prayers are taken from letters and articles included in *The Collected Works*. A glossary has been added to explain names and terms unfamiliar to western readers. Hymn numbers from the original edition are shown at the end of each prayer.

We would like to express our thanks to the Navajivan Trust, Ahmedabad, India for their assistance and permission to reprint this work; to Linda Hess for help in developing the glossary; and to Vandana Shiva and Eknath Easwaran who, through their ideas and writings, first planted the seeds of this project.

Foreword

ARUN GANDHI

I attended many of Grandfather's prayer meetings at Sevagram Ashram in Wardha, Central India, and also when he traveled to various places between 1945 and 1947. His prayer services always intrigued me because they were so unlike the prayers that I had witnessed elsewhere. Ordinarily people either went to ornate temples, churches, synagogues and mosques, or performed an assortment of rituals at home. Even to a thirteen-year-old it was quite apparent that worship and prayers were centered on money.

What was different about Grandfather's way of worship was the inclusiveness and simplicity. Every morning and evening we would assemble in an open field where a few hundred people could squat on grass or even on dirt to participate in a truly interfaith experience. People who came belonged to different faiths, and even no faith. There were Muslims, Hindus, Christians, Sikhs, Jews, agnostics, atheists and others, because Gandhi's prayers were an attempt to search for the truth. Everyone participated without reservations or inhibitions.

Through these inclusive prayers, what Grandfather attempted to do was to foster respect for different faiths and show people, through personal example, that religion must be a unifying force rather than a divisive force. Religion must bring people together through understanding and respect, like children who pursue different vocations but gather for a family reunion in the home of their parents.

Religions today have become far too competitive. Each vies with the other to assert its superiority and proclaim itself to be the only way. Yet, in reality, no religion is perfect. The tragedy lies in our basic understanding of religion. Our attitude is conditioned by whether we believe we *possess* the truth or we believe we *pursue* the truth. If we accept the premise that we pursue the truth, then it becomes easier to accept and respect different forms of worship and philosophies. The alternative is too grim to even contemplate—a terrible holocaust perpetrated in the name of religion.

This book of prayers, personally selected and translated into the English language by Grandfather, is a big step towards understanding the true meaning of religion and salvation. I hope the reader finds the peace in these pages that Grandfather found every day of his life.

Introduction

MICHAEL N. NAGLER

In May of 1930, Gandhi was in prison for launching the famous "Salt Satyagraha," which convulsed India and, as we know in retrospect, sealed the ultimate departure of the British raj. The Mahatma was at the height of his power. He had returned to his native country from a twenty-one-year sojourn in South Africa with the discovery of satyagraha, his nonviolent method of struggle, and its success at gaining basic rights for the Indian community there, solidly behind him. After a year of silence, he had quickly moved center stage as the voice of India's liberation from colonial abuses, forging the dormant All-India Congress into a powerful political instrument. Then, when London defaulted on its assurances of greater freedom for India after the Great War, he had launched mass civil disobedience campaigns, which only stopped when he himself suspended them for Indian breaches of nonviolence.

After reflection and soul-searching, Gandhi had hit upon the grossly unfair British monopoly on salt as the issue that could reinvigorate the struggle for self-determination. He had marched some 240 miles down to the sea at Dandi, in northwest India, to harvest "illegal" salt, and millions of his countrymen had responded enthusiastically. Freedom must have finally seemed within their grasp, and to be thrown into jail just then might have been unbearable, especially since Gandhi, on principle, never carried on political activity from behind bars.

The Mahatma, however, had learned to make good use of his prison terms for rest, writing and study. Some ten years earlier, he had read no less than 150 books before being released from the same jail, Yeravda Central Prison. This time he decided to translate into English the *Ashram Bhajanavali*, the book of prayers and devotional songs, which the residents of his spiritual community, Satyagraha Ashram, used in their morning and evening worship. He did this translation at the request of Mirabehn, a.k.a. Madeleine Slade, a British Admiral's daughter and one of his closest followers, but he was aware that it might be read by thousands throughout India, and indeed by posterity—by us.

Since Mirabehn needed no translations of the dozen or so Christian hymns in use at the ashram, none appear in Gandhi's collection (two of his favorite Christian lyrics are provided here in an Appendix). The inclusion, however, of Moslem, Jain and Sikh verses reflects the universality of Gandhi's religion. Squarely in the time-honored tradition of Hindu devotion, Gandhi accepted the validity of all forms of genuine worship. Love of God is love of God. At the same time, he explained, we need forms suited to our culture and even to our personality; since most of the ashramites were Hindu, so are most of the songs. Indeed, most of them are translated from Gujarati, the language of Gandhi's native region where the Satyagraha Ashram was located. He was quick to point out that this should be no obstacle to worshippers of other faiths. The unprejudiced devotee can touch the joy and inspiration in these songs no matter what his or her denomination.

In the collection of essays, *Ashram Observances in Action*, Gandhi describes how the hymns, *bhajans*, translated here were actually used. Morning prayers began at 4:20 A.M. That early hour was fixed on after much groaning and protestation, and was only settled, as he dryly puts it, "on account of my persistently strong attitude on the subject." We get a glimpse of Gandhi the man here— there were few subjects on which he did not have a "persistently strong attitude." But, in addition, this suggests the importance he attributed to this practice. Early morning is when the mind is freshest, most impressionable and most amenable to discipline. Very early morning and also evening, dawn and dusk, those liminal moments which sages have called the *sandhya* or "junction" of day and night, were fixed upon as the best times for meditation thousands of years ago. There was more to hymn-singing than spiritual fellowship.

This is the program one would have seen upon visiting Satyagraha Ashram in the early 1930s, whether Gandhi himself was present, away on some campaign, or sojourning in His Majesty's prison:

At the morning prayer we first recite the *shlokas* (verses) printed in *Ashram Bhajanavali*, and then sing one *bhajan*, followed by *ramdhun* (repetition of the name of God, Rama) and *gitapath* (recitation of verses from the Bhagavad Gita). In the evening we have recitation of the last nineteen verses of the second chapter of the Gita, one *bhajan* and *ramdhun,* and then read some portion of a sacred book. . . . Since the ashram was founded, not a single day has passed to my knowledge without this worship.

Why, one might wonder, take the time to do all this in the middle of a revolution? Gandhi was not one to cling to empty forms. An answer may be found in the testimony of someone who observed Gandhi during one of those evening prayers. As you read it, bear in mind that the nineteen verses of the second chapter of the Gita, the description of the illumined man, is widely regarded as the Sermon on the Mount of Hinduism

The sun had set when we got back [from his regular evening walk]. Hurricane lanterns were lit; Gandhi settled down at the base of a neem tree as ashramites and the rest of us huddled in. Some hymns were sung, then Gandhi's secretary began reciting the second chapter of the . . . Bhagavad Gita. Then it happened.

Not that I can describe it very easily. Gandhi's eyes closed; his body went stock still; it seemed as though centuries had rolled away and I was seeing the Buddha in a living person. I saw what we had almost forgotten was possible in the modern world: a man who had conquered himself to the extent that some force greater than a human being . . . moved through him and affected everyone.

Even though Gandhi was not off in some solitary cave, even though he was not shutting his ears to outside sounds, we can hardly fail to recognize that this is deep meditation. Sri Easwaran, a young student at the time that he witnessed the above transfiguration, had gone to the ashram to find for himself the answer to a simple question: what was the source of this man's power? How had he shaken up a subcontinent full of demoralized people, cowed down by fear, and set them on the road that leads, through incredible struggle and defiance and sacrifice, to freedom? He got his answer. Gandhi had the power to shake India, in part, because he drew on re- sources within himself that are not normally accessible. And that access happened, among other occasions, at the high point of these prayer meetings. "In heartfelt prayer," Gandhi confirms, "the worshipper's attention is concen- trated on the object of worship so much so that he is not conscious of anything else besides." That is a clue to the power of the prayer meetings, and their significance to the intense struggle whirling around that quiet ashram.

There is a tendency to think that meditation and action are opposites, that one chooses between one way of life or the other. But as the Bhagavad Gita insists, medi- tation and selfless action are inseparable. They are oppo- site sides of the same coin, as complementary as breath- ing in and breathing out. They not only do not exclude each other, they need each other. By reaching normally untapped inner resources, one can unleash the energy needed to make major changes in one's self and others, and the wisdom to guide that energy. Meditation enables one to act without the contaminant of selfish attachment. That applies with particular force when the action in question happens to be a revolution.

Far from being a distraction, then, the devotional practices of the ashram were the very stuff of revolution. For Gandhi there was no distinction whatever between the social purpose of the community—to raise India and in the process shake off her colonial chains—and the spiritual purpose which has always been the center of ashram life—to raise the consciousness of individuals by shaking off their egocentric chains. "Politics without religion," he wrote, "is mere dirt."

I like to illustrate this connection between the spiritual and the political with an episode from the civil rights struggle here in the United States. It was in Birmingham, Alabama, in 1964. A peaceful march was making its way towards city hall to protest the lack of voting rights when it was suddenly stopped by a cohort of police and firemen with dogs and hoses ready. Taken unawares, the marchers decided to kneel down and pray. After a short while, in the words of one witness, they became "spiritually intoxicated." Acting as one, they got up on their feet and started moving again, right into the blockade. The sheriff, a notorious segregationist, yelled, "Turn on the hoses." Once again he ordered, "Turn on the hoses!" but strangely the firemen did not—could not—obey. The marchers passed right through them unobstructed. "How do you feel about what you're doing?" some said to the police and firemen. Witnesses say even the dogs were quiet.

The purpose of the ashram was to train people to be a little spiritually intoxicated all the time. In times of relative peace, they could give themselves over to the quieter practices of self-realization; in times of struggle (and when were they not?) they could actively confront the forces of darkness around them. And so, as Gandhi translated the ashram prayer book in the prison he called Yeravda Mandir, Yeravda Temple, observing the letter of his self-imposed rule to refrain from political work while jailed, he was, in fact doing politics of the deepest kind, making changes that are good for all time—by elevating human consciousness.

This edition of *Ashram Bhajanavali* is a selection of 108 prayers from the 253 originally translated by Gandhi and published in his collected works. We were influenced somewhat in our choices by the sacredness of the number 108 in Hinduism. But essentially, there is nothing "Hindu" about these beautiful offerings of praise, and Gandhi would hardly mind knowing that thousands of others, of many faiths, are reading them today in the country where his successor, Martin Luther King, Jr., lived and died. Whatever may be lost in the translation from India then to here and now, should be more than compensated for by the fact that this is no ordinary translator, but someone who made the truths of these prayers a daily lived reality.

Gandhi was no poet, he claimed. He described himself, rather, as a "practical idealist," a "humble seeker after truth," and a man who had "ceased for over forty years to hate anyone on earth." But those are very poetic claims, in a sense—the claims of a man who lived with high artistry. And one can't help recognizing that these *bhajans*, translated roughly one per day for a beloved disciple, evoked some of his deepest creativity.

In the early morning I worship him
who is beyond the reach
of thought and speech,
and yet by whose grace all speech is possible. (2)

God is everywhere, he fills his creation.
Among the movable and the immovable objects
there is not an atom but has his presence in it.
He is like the heavens pervading all.
He is like the air inhabiting my heart. . . .
Brahma and his creation cannot be separated even
    for a moment,
but we, of the earth earthy, have no inkling of that
    vital principle;
an owl may live for a hundred years
and still will not know what the day is like. (252)

Alongside the universality of these truths and the simplicity of the imagery that conveys them are cultural elements embedded in specifically Hindu associations. For these, a few words of explanation might be helpful.

The first part of the ashram's prayer service drew upon verses from the ancient Sanskrit Upanishads and Vedas, the earliest documents of any length from an Indo-European people. Verses from this class of ancient religious poetry are sometimes referred to as *mantras*. (This is not to be confused with a mantram, the divine formula recited by millions of Hindus and not a few Westerners.) These verses have an evocative power for Indians which is difficult to appreciate in our young, polyglot civilization. They are widely regarded as words of reality itself, not composed by human beings but "seen" by sages in the depths of contemplation. They are extremely familiar to Indians, and yet thrilling. In prayer 38, for example, taken from the Mundaka Upanishad, the phrase, "Truth alone triumphs, never untruth," *(Satyam eva jayate, nntam)* is the motto of modern India.

After these mantras, which represent about the first fifth of the *Ashram Bhajanavali*, come hymns from the Hindi, Gujarati and Bengali languages that represent very well the *bhakti* tradition, the intensely devotional religion of modern Hinduism. "Give thyself to devotion and merge thyself in God. Let people say what they like; for this, thou shouldst store up overwhelming love." (185) What breathes here is not too dissimilar to the spirit of the Psalms, if one looks for a familiar comparison. Occasionally, too, the Psalms rise to a kind of mysticism, and to a kind of nonviolent religion one might associate with Gandhi. "Let the righteous smite me; it shall be a kindness: and let him reprove me; it shall be an excellent oil." (Ps. 141). But the modern Hindu casts her or his devotion in a much more folksy rhetoric, taking liberties with God that would shock the ancient Israelites. "Be thou warned, O my protector, thy prestige will be lost if anything happens to thy servant!" (233).

These songs—and *bhajans* were always sung, there is almost no merely recited poetry in traditional India—often end with a signature line identifying their author-composer. Many westerners will recognize some of these names—Mira, the Rajput princess who forsook throne and family to raise high the banner of the love of God; Kabir, the humble weaver whose vast body of devotional songs became scripture for what is practically a distinct religion, merging Hindu and Muslim elements and imagery; and Tulsidas, whose translation of the Ramayana into the vernacular had such inestimable influence and was Gandhi's Bible, alongside the Bhagavad Gita. A glossary at the end of this collection provides a few particulars for many of these poets.

As a Native American informant once told a researcher, "Our songs are short because we know so much." In the same way, the prayers of Satyagraha Ashram often allude to well-known stories, and these allusions, although quite brief, are tremendously important because these stories have been for so long part of the thinking process of the Indian people. Education scholar William Kilpatrick reminds us, "Morality needs to be set within a storied vision." Children and adults alike, he argues, learn how to behave from stories far more pointedly than they ever do from the admonitions of elders, from pulpit or classroom or philosophy. India has always conveyed culture through stories, of which a vast repertoire is preserved in forms which remain close to oral tradition. One that recurs powerfully in this collection is the rescue of Queen Draupadi.

Draupadi's story is, in my opinion, the key and plot-driver of that vast and definitive epic which is the Mahabharata. To make it un-Indianly short, Draupadi has been lost as a piece of property to the enemies of her five husbands in a crooked dice match. Those five great warriors are powerless to protect her as their enemies prepare to humiliate her by stripping off her sari in front of the entire court. Draupadi cries out for protection from her Lord. Counter to expectation, though, the Lord does nothing. Even his divine consort complains to him, "Is this how you protect your devotees?" He then shows her where Draupadi is raising one hand to him in supplication, but clutching her sari with the other. "She doesn't need my help." It is only after a struggle of unendurable suspense that Draupadi lets go of her sari and raises both hands to God for help. For a moment we endure another shock as the sari begins to spool off under the eager hands of her assailant, but after the traditional six yards the rich silk goes on and on, reeling off yard after yard until her attacker, the ill-fated Duhshasana, sinks down exhausted and his cohorts grind their teeth in frustration. Like all great myth, Draupadi's story continues to speak to us.

My first exposure to India's rich heritage of religious songs was through a visiting scholar from India, whom I heard interviewed by a Professor at Berkeley in the mid 1960s, when I was still a graduate student. The Professor was being perfectly obtuse in his questions and paraphrases, which annoyed me no end, and I remember to this day how the Indian scholar finally got exasperated and said, "You know, what you're saying might be true, but the simplest peasant in village India, even if he's illiterate, will know thousands upon thousands of hymns by heart."

The Professor— an anthropologist, no less—quickly changed the subject. I was outraged, but at the time, my objections were esthetic and political. Little did I realize how, thirty years later, these traditional Indian lyrics would come to mean much more to me than simply good poetry, or the authentic voice of a third-world people. At that time I had little inkling what it could mean to grow up in a rich and positive culture where the human being is held to have such an intimate relation to the divine.

Rationalists, as many of us style ourselves, may find it hard to relate to images of Sarasvati, "white as the *mogra* flower or the moon and a garland of snow . . . seated on a white lotus," but as Gandhi explains,

> I claim to be a votary of truth, and yet I do not mind reciting these verses or teaching them to the children. . . . I do not believe that this [mythological symbolism] is a weak or vulnerable point of Hinduism. Sarasvati and Ganesh are not independent entities. They are all descriptive names of one God. Devoted poets have given a local habitation and a name to his count-

less attributes. They have done nothing wrong.

Indeed, Gandhi would go further. In a letter to Mirabehn written shortly after completing these translations, he writes,

> These imaginary gods are more real than the so-called real things we perceive with our five senses. When I recite this verse (5), for instance, I never think that I am addressing an imaginary picture. The recitation is a mystical act. That when I analyze the act intellectually, I know the goddess is an imaginary being, does not in any way affect the value of the recitation at prayer time.

When Gandhi fell to his assassin's bullets in 1948, the last words to pass his lips were, "He Rama." This was, of course, his mantram, which his nurse, Rambha, had taught him to use when he was a boy, afraid of his own shadow. Here it is uttered, we might say, in triumph, as a last benediction on all those around him—even the man who stood before him, pistol still shaking in his hand. In order for the mantram to rise from such depths that he was able to say it with his last breath, he must have repeated it reverently, tirelessly, for seven decades.

If not quite as deeply as his mantram, the hymns in this collection were also woven into the content of Gandhi's consciousness, just as the Psalms of David became the grammar of St. Augustine's mind—as anyone knows who has perused an annotated edition of his *Con-*

fessions. Augustine doesn't even realize he is quoting the Psalms, it sometimes seems; he is thinking in them. Inevitably, then, in course of time he began acting them out. So Gandhi, too, would allude to or "think in" lines from these hymns in the course of some discussion or other. Their images and stories are part of the lexicon of his world view. Prayer 178, for example, the prayer of Narasimha Mehta, was so often on his lips and in his heart that you can almost see him molding himself on that ideal of the true lover of God who "feels another's sorrows as his own."

I am among those who believe that Mahatma Gandhi is the most indispensable human being of the twentieth century; that, as Martin Luther King, Jr. said, "We ignore him at our peril." It is the inner man, about which the least is known, that makes him most indispensable, for his prayer life lay at the root of all his social experiments. For those of us who would follow him there, these hymns are a most precious legacy. They join Gandhi's vernacular translation of the Bhagavad Gita, and the Ramayana, to form what he described as "those three shields to protect us. . . . I believe, and I want you all to believe, that the constant reading of these, with faith, will be a greater source of strength than letters from me, or living with me." Perhaps he was exaggerating, or perhaps this was an expression of humility; nonetheless these hymns were, and are, close to the heart of the man we now sorely lack.

Book of Prayers

Early in the morning I call to mind
that being which is felt in the heart
which is *sat, chit* and *sukham,*
the eternal, knowledge and bliss,
which is the state reached by perfect men,
and which is the super-state.

I am that immaculate Brahma
which ever notes the states of dream,
wakefulness and deep sleep,
not this body, the compound made of
the elements—earth, water, space, light and air.

(I)

Note: "Formerly I used to shudder to utter this verse thinking
that the claim made therein was arrogant. But when I saw the
meaning more clearly, I perceived at once that it was the very best
thought with which to commence the day. It is a solemn declara-
tion that we are not the changeful bodies which require sleep,
etc., but deep down, we are the Being, the witness pervading the
countless bodies." M.K.G.

In the early morning I worship him
who is beyond the reach
of thought and speech,
and yet by whose grace all speech is possible.
I worship him whom the Vedas describe
as *neti, neti*—not this, not this.
Him they, the sages, have called
God of gods, the unborn,
the unfallen, the source of all.

(2)

In the early morning I bow to him
who is beyond darkness,
who is like the sun,
who is perfect, ancient,
called Purushottama, the best among men,
and in whom, through the veil of darkness,
we fancy the whole universe as appearing,
even as, in darkness,
we imagine a rope to be a snake.

(3)

Note: "The idea is that the universe is not real in the sense of being permanent; it is neither a thing to be harkened after nor feared because it is supposed to be God's creation. As a matter of fact, it is a creation of our imagination even as the snake in the rope is. The real universe, like the real rope, is there. We perceive neither when the veil is lifted and darkness is gone. Compare 'And with the morn, those angel faces smile which I have loved long since and lost awhile.'" M.K.G. (cf. page 144)

O! goddess Earth
with the ocean for thy garment,
mountains for thy breasts,
thou consort of Vishnu, the Preserver,
I bow to thee.
Forgive the touch of my feet.

(4)

Note: "We are of the earth earthy. If earth is not, we are not. I feel nearer God by feeling him through the earth. In bowing to the earth, I at once realize my indebtedness to Him, and if I am a worthy child of that Mother, I shall at once reduce myself to dust and rejoice in establishing kinship with not only the lowliest of human beings, but also with lowest forms of creation, whose fate—reduction to dust—I have to share with them." M.K.G.

May the goddess of learning, Sarasvati,
the destroyer completely of black ignorance,
protect me—
she who is white as the *mogra* flower
or the moon and a garland of snow,
who has worn white robes,
whose hands are adorned
with the beautiful bamboo of her *veena*,
who is seated on a white lotus
and who is always adored
by Brahma, Vishnu, Siva and the other gods.

(5)

Note: "The emphasis on threefold whiteness, that of snowy
moon, flower and the white dress and white seat is intended to
show that uttermost purity is an indispensable part of wisdom
or learning." M.K.G.

Guru is Brahma,
he is Vishnu,
he is Mahadev,
he is the great Brahman itself.
I bow to that guru.

(7)

Note: "This refers of course to the spiritual teacher. This is not
a mechanical or artificial relationship. The teacher is not all these
in reality, but he is all that to the disciple who finds his full
satisfaction in him and imputes perfection to him, who gave him
living faith in a living God. Such a guru is a rarity, at least nowa-
days. The best thing is to think of God Himself as one's guru, or
await the Light in faith." M.K.G.

Blessed be the people.
May the rulers protect
their kingdoms by just means.
May it be always well
with the cow and the brahmin.
May all the peoples be happy.

(11)

Note: "Cow = agriculture; Brahmin = Education" M.K.G.

That which goes by the name of adversity is not such;
nor is that prosperity which goes by that name.
To forget God is adversity;
ever to think of him is prosperity.

(16)

Note: "Realising our littleness during this tiny span of life, we close every morning prayer with the recitation of [this] verse." M.K.G.

Let him be whosoever he may be
whether Vishnu or Mahadev,
Brahma or Indra,
Sun or Moon,
Lord Buddha or Mahavir—
obeisance be ever only to him
who is free from the poisonous effect
of desire and anger,
who is filled with compassion for all life,
and who is purified by a perfectly virtuous life.

(17)

Those knowing ones who, with austerities and faith
live the forest life in peace, begging for their food,
becoming sinless, enter through the sunny gate
that abode where dwells immortal, changeless being.

(23)

Regard the soul as the warrior, body as his chariot,
reason as the charioteer, mind as the reins;
they call senses horses, sense-objects meadows;
wise men have said that the soul
acts through the mind and the senses.

He whose reason is like an experienced charioteer
and whose mind is under control like the reins
crosses over safely, and safely comes to
the journey's end, the excellent abode of Vishnu.

(24-25)

Even as fire, though always the same, assumes different forms as it passes through different media, so does the indwelling spirit, though essentially always the same, appear different passing through different media.

Even as the air, though always the same, assumes different forms as it passes through different media, so does the indwelling spirit, though essentially always the same, appear different passing through different media.

Even as the sun, which gives light to all the eyes, remains unaffected by the external defects of these eyes, so is the oversoul dwelling in all that lives not affected by the external woes of mankind.

Those wise men alone, not others, attain eternal happiness, who feel dwelling in themselves that one all-controlling power which pervades all life and, though one, appears as many.

Those wise men alone, not others, attain eternal peace, who feel dwelling in themselves that God who is the permanent essence among the impermanent, who is the life in all that lives, and who, though one, fulfills the desires of many.

(27-30)

Self-realization comes always through truth,
austerity, true knowledge and self-restraint.
Seekers who have become free from sins realize
the immaculate refulgent spirit within themselves.

Truth alone triumphs, never untruth.
That way which the sages whose purpose is fulfilled
     traverse,
which is the way of the gods,
and which is the great abode of truth,
opens for us through truth.

(37-38)

Just as rivers rushing towards the sea
leave their names and forms and merge in the sea,
even so do wise men leave their names and forms
and merge in the paramount divine being.

He who knows that great Brahman becomes It.
In his family no one ignorant of Brahman is possible.
He passes grief and sin. He becomes free
from the bonds of the heart and becomes immortal.

(43-44)

Soul-force is superior even to science,
for one man having soul-force
will shake one hundred learned men.
When one has that force he is ready to go to a teacher,
he serves him, then he becomes fit to sit near him,
he ponders over what he has heard; he becomes wise,
he does his duty, he has experience.
The earth keeps its place through that force,
the heavens retain their place through it,
the mountains, the gods, mankind, the brute creation,
birds, grass, plants, game, insects, moths, ants,
all life are sustained by that force.
Therefore cultivate that force.

(48)

May the winds, the waters, the plant life,
the evening and the dawn,
the dust of the earth,
the heavenly vault which is like father,
the trees, the sun and the cows
be a blessing to us.

(49)

One may not abandon one's faith
for the satisfaction of a desire,
or from fear or ambition,
not even for saving one's life.
Faith is permanent,
happiness and unhappiness are fleeting things.
The spirit is immortal,
the result of its actions—the body—is evanescent.

(50)

O*m!*

May God protect us,
may he support us,
may we make joint progress,
may our studies be fruitful,
may we never harbour ill will
against one another.

Om shanti, shanti, shanti.

(53)

Om!

From untruth lead me unto truth,
from darkness lead me unto light,
from death lead me unto life everlasting.

(54)

Note: This prayer was sung on January 18, 1948 as Gandhi broke his final fast, which he had undertaken to bring an end to waves of violence between Hindus, Moslems and other religious groups throughout India. India had gained her independence five months earlier. Gandhi was seventy-eight years old. He was assasinated seven days later by a Hindu fundamentalist as he was about to begin a public prayer meeting.

Act righteously, never unrighteously;
speak truth, never untruth;
look far ahead, never shortsightedly;
look above, never below.

(57)

Ahimsa, truth, non-stealing, purity and self-control,
these, said Manu, are the common duty of all the four
    divisions.

Ahimsa, truth, non-stealing, freedom from passion,
    anger and greed,
wishing the well-being and good of all that lives,
these are the duty common to all the divisions.

(58-59)

Listen to the essence of religion
and assimilate it through the heart:
one should never do to others
which one would not wish done to oneself.
That which has been said in countless books
I shall say in half a verse:
service of others is virtue, injury to others is sin.

(61)

O Mukunda!
With head bowed down I ask of thee only this: that by thy grace, I may never, from birth to death, lose sight of thy lotus feet.

O God!
I have no relish for dharma, nor for wealth, nor yet for worldly enjoyments; let whatever is to happen happen as a result of my past actions. Only this prayer I regard as of utmost importance: may my attachment to thy lotus feet be unshakable.

O thou destroyer of hell!
I do not care where my lot is to be cast, whether in heaven or on earth or in hell. Only grant that I may ever think of thy feet, more beautiful than the lotus during the rains.

(74)

O my heart!
You need not be afraid that you cannot cross this unfathomable and difficult ocean of birth and death; thy single-minded devotion to the lotus-eyed, hell-destroying God will surely save thee.

O Lotus-eyed One!
With hands folded, head bowed, body moved, throat choked, eyes bathed in hot tears, may our life close ever drinking in nectar in the form of meditation on thy lotus-like feet.

O Cupid!
Get thee gone from my heart, which is the seat of the lotus-like feet of Mukunda. Thou art already scorched by the fire from Siva's eyes; why will you not remember the might of Vishnu's discus?

O thou wrong-headed fool!
Why dost thou afflict with drugs this body, which has hundreds of weak joints, which is liable to certain decay and which is subject to constant change? Drink in the one life-giving potion—the name of Krishna.

(75)

For those in want there is no other than thou
so merciful, so generous!
What is the use of my carrying my wants to others?
They appear to me as much in want as myself.
Gods, men, sages, demons, serpents and others
exercise sway only during thy pleasure.
The world, eternity, the four Vedas proclaim
that Rama is the beginning, the end and the middle.
Thine is the kingdom. To ask of thee is not begging.
Thy devotee comes to thee for thy well-known nature;
for hast thou not taken under thy protection
stone, beast, trees, bird?
O thou, son of Lord Dasharatha,
thou hast turned beggars into kings,
thou art the refuge of the distressed.
I am thy slave.
O merciful God, say, if only once, "Tulsidas is mine."

(78)

Thou art merciful, I am in distress;
thou art the giver, I am a beggar;
I am a known sinner, thou art the forgiver of mountains
of sins;
thou art the help of the helpless, and who can be so
helpless as I?
There is none so afflicted like me, there is no deliverer
like unto thee;
thou art the creator, I am a little creature;
thou art the lord, I am a slave;
thou art father, brother, teacher, friend, all in all to me.
If I have only faith, I know that there is much between
thee and me.
May Tulsi somehow feel the protecting power of thy
holy feet.

(79)

When shall I conduct myself thus
by the grace of the merciful Rama:
that I shall cultivate the nature of good and true men;
that I shall be satisfied with whatever accrues to me
in the ordinary course and shall expect nothing from
     anybody;
that I shall carry out the resolution to serve others
in thought, deed and word;
that I shall not burn with the scorching fire
of the unbearably harsh language of others
when I chance to hear it;
that I shall be free from pride and have a mind equipoised,
and not delight in narrating the defects of others,
and that I shall give up all anxiety about the body,
and will not be elated by happiness and downcast by
     misery?
Tulsidas declares, Being steadfast along the foregoing path
I shall attain the boon of unchangeable devotion.

(80)

O Lord! Hear this my prayer.
Remove my ignorance which makes me cherish
expectations of, and faith in, others rather than thee.
I want neither heaven, nor good intellect,
nor riches, nor possessions, nor greatness.
I want an ever-growing devotion to thee
without expectation of reward.
May thy grace save me, even as the tortoise its eggs,
from succumbing to the weakness of my irresistible
evil nature. Tulsidas prays for deliverance
from all egotism and attachments of the body.

(82)

O Raghuvir, help of the distressed,
to whom shall I take the tale of my great misery?
My heart, O my God, is thy abode,
but many thieves have entered therein,
and although I am beseeching and imploring them
to leave it, they are using unbearable force.
Ignorance, delusion, greed, pride, arrogance, anger,
    passion—
all enemies of free knowledge—
are causing much trouble, O Lord,
and thinking me to be helpless are crushing me.
I am alone, the thieves are many, no one hears my cries;
Lord, there is no escape from this either.
O Lord of the Raghus, protect me.
Tulsidas says,
Listen, O Rama, thieves are looting thy house;
my great anxiety is lest they should bring discredit on
    thee!

(84)

What should I do to be able to pray?
I am afraid, for looking at my conduct
I realize my defeat.
I obstinately refrain from doing the things
which make God merciful towards his devotees,
and I follow the path that leads me into
the trap of misfortune and daily misery.
I know that I should be safe if I gave myself
in thought, word and deed
to the service of fellow creatures,
but on the contrary
I am vainly jealous when I see others happy.
The Vedas, the Puranas and other scriptures
proclaim the necessity of cultivating firmly
the companionship of the good,
but my pride, passion and jealousy
turn me away from them.
I always delight in that which will lead me unto misery.
Now tell me, O Lord!
how may I be delivered from this misery?
I can only be saved if thou, according to thy nature,
will have mercy on me.
Tulsidas has no other hope;
how long shall he remain in this mire?

(87)

O Prince of the Raghus, wake up.
The birds are singing in the grove,
the moon will disappear presently,
the *chakravaka* bird is off to meet her lord,
the threefold breeze is gently blowing,
the leaves are rustling,
the morning sun is on the horizon,
darkness of the night is gone,
the bees are humming,
the lotus has opened its leaf,
Brahma and others are in meditation,
the gods, common people and sages
are singing hymns of praise.
Thus when it was rising time Rama opened his eyes.
Tulsidas is overjoyed to see the lotus face of Rama,
who gives valuables as gifts to the poor.

(90)

I have spoiled everything hitherto
but will do so no longer.
By the grace of God the night is past,
I am awake and shall no more go to sleep.
I have the talisman in the shape of God's name.
It shall not vanish from my heart.
The beautiful and holy face of God is the testing stone,
The gold of my heart shall be tested on it.
My sense organs finding me without control
have mocked me. I have now acquired self-control,
they shall no more deride me.
My mind, like the bee on the lotus,
shall lean on the lotus feet of Rama.

(94)

In the *Kaliyuga*, Ramanama is the all-yielding tree.
It is the destroyer of scorching miseries
caused by bad times and pauperism.
Repeating the name purifies the mind and banishes
      misfortune.
Valmiki and Shankar sing the virtues of taking the name,
whether correctly or with the letters transposed.
It is well here and hereafter with those who are armed
with the beautiful power of the name.
Tulsi says: I am able to live in the world peacefully
by the power of the name. I have no anxiety
whether I live or die.

(97)

I have heard that Rama is the help of the helpless.
I can produce the evidence of those saintly people
who were helped by him in their adversity.
So long as the elephant relied upon his own strength,
his case was hopeless, but when in his helplessness
he invoked the assistance of Rama, he responded
when hardly his name was half pronounced.
When Draupadi felt helpless, he felt the call in his seat
and, God having multiplied her clothing, Dushasana
grew tired of hopelessly trying to strip her naked.
Man relies on his own strength, or his austerities,
or the strength of his arms, or fourthly his wealth.
Surdas says that when a man has exhausted
all his resources and invokes the name of God,
His grace descends upon him.

(103)

Who can be so crooked, bad or dissolute as I?
I am so faithless that I have forgotten
the very God who gave me this body.
Even like the village dog
I have been fattening myself and running after pleasures.
I have given up the company of God's people,
and day and night slave for those who revile him.
Who can be a greater sinner than I?
I am the chief among them.
Surdas says, O God, listen,
where is the resting place for a sinner like me?

(106)

O Gopal,
I have danced away my life in self-indulgence.
Desire and anger were my garment,
passions were my garland,
infatuation was my ankle-bells,
backbiting was the sweet sounding tune,
poisoned mind was the tabor,
evil company was the step,
insatiableness was the accompanying measure
of various kind, *maya* was the waist-band,
ambition was the mark on my forehead
and I showed much cunning—
so much so that I forgot all about time or place.
Surdas says, O Nandalal,
remove all this ignorance of mine.

(110)

Although Putna administered poison to Krishna
she attained salvation; the Vedas have sung in vain
that man reaps as he sows.
King Bali performed a hundred sacrifices
and yet was tied up and sent to the nether world.
King Nriga donated ten million cows
and yet he was turned into a serpent.
Friend Sudama was born a pauper
and suddenly found himself in a golden palace.
Surdas, says, O God, strange are thy ways.
Well have the Vedas said, "Not this, not this."

(113)

Open thy face, thou wilt see thy beloved.
He is in everyone, therefore say nothing bitter of
    anyone.
Do not brag about thy riches or youth;
this case made of five elements will play false to thee
    one day.
Light up thy dark heart and do not move from thy
    purpose.
Wake up in this temple, for thou hast got the priceless
    treasure, thy Lord.
Kabir says, Let there be rejoicing, for the Lord's voice is
    heard within.

(117)

O good man, natural meditation is best.
Ever since its manifestation, by the grace of God, it has
    waxed.
Wherever I wander, it is a circuit round a temple,
whatever I do is for service,
whenever I lie down, it is my prostration before God.
I worship no other god but God.
Whatever I utter, it is God's name,
whatever I hear is a remembrance of God.
My eating and drinking are worship,
whether a home is established or it is destroyed is the
    same thing to me.
I do not allow any other feeling to possess me.
I do not shut my eyes nor stuff my ears, I do not
    torture the body.
I open my eyes and delight to see God and contemplate
    his beauty.
My mind is ever intent on him; all corrupt thought has
    left me.
I am so much engrossed in the thought of him that I
    think of him whatever I am doing.
Kabir says, This is the excellent life and I have sung of it.
There is a state beyond misery and happiness, my mind
    is fixed on it.

(118)

We are not to stay here long,
it is a foreign land for us.
The world is like a paper parcel
which is reduced to pulp
on a little water being poured on it,
or it is like a hedge of thorns
in which we get entangled and die,
or it is like a meadow full of shrubs and grass
which a fire destroys in no time.
Kabir says, Listen all ye good people,
the only safety lies in
seeking the protection of God.

(120)

O friend, my mind is fixed on a fakir's life.
The happiness which one derives from meditation
    on God
is not to be found in indulgence.
Bear whatever befalls thee—good and evil.
Live in poverty.
Let us live a life of loving service.
It will be well to cultivate patience.
When one goes about with a mere begging bowl and
a staff, one has the whole world as one's kingdom.
What is the use of pride when one realizes
that the body is soon to be reduced to ashes?
Kabir says, Listen O ye all good men,
contentment is the pathway to self-realization.

(121)

Be thou absorbed in God, let the world go its way.
There is paper and there is black ink, let those who
    wish write or read.
The elephant does not abandon its gait despite the
    barkings of dogs.
Kabir says, Listen O ye good men,
those who are intent upon evil will go their way.

(123)

Without the Master, who can show the path?
The way is terribly difficult.
Doubt crosses the path like rivers
gliding through mountainous regions,
and there is egotism like big boulders in the rivers.
There are, too, passion and anger
like two huge mountains on either side;
ambition dogs the footsteps like a thief,
and pride and vanity descend like rain
from overhanging clouds;
self-deception violently tosses one like the winds.
Kabir says, Listen O ye good men,
how can one traverse the path without a Master as
    guide?

(125)

O Father, I will not give up Ramanama. I have nothing to do with the other lessons.

The King sent Prahlad to school and he had many companions. He said, "Why do you teach me nonsense? Write on my slate Shri Gopal." This Shandamara duly reported, and the King immediately sent for Prahlad to whom he said, "Leave thou the name of Rama. If thou wilt do what I tell thee, I will set thee free." Prahlad replied, "Why vex me again and again. God made the ocean, the earth, the sky and the mountain. I swear by my guru that I will not give up Ramanama. You may burn me, you may bury me alive, you may kill me anyway you choose."

On this the King was enraged, drew his sword and challenged Prahlad to show his deliverer. God in his might rose from the pillar of fire and with his paws killed the King.

O great one, God of gods, thou becamest Narasinha for the sake of thy devotee. Kabir says, I can fill pages with the stories of how he delivered Prahlad from many a danger.

(126)

What is the use of taking pride
either in this body or in wealth?
They vanish in the twinkling of an eye.
A man builds a palace himself and is often obliged to
    take refuge in the woods.
On death, the bones will burn like faggots and hair like
    grass.
Kabir says, O virtuous people, listen—
when man dies, all his airy castles crumble to pieces.

(128)

O God, I seek refuge in thee.
On seeing thee, all my doubts have disappeared.
Without my mentioning it, thou hast known my
   trouble.
Thou hast made me remember thee.
My misery is gone and I am all happiness.
Joyfully do I sing thy praise.
Thou hast taken me by the arm
and pulled me safe out of the dark well of *maya*.
Nanak says,
The Lord has removed my bondage
and brought me back, though I had strayed away.

(133)

O God, ever since I have had the companionship of
     the good,
the distinction between mine and thine has disappeared.
I deem no one as enemy or stranger.
I am on friendly terms with everyone.
From the good I have learnt to consider as good
whatever comes from God.
Nanak takes delight in finding that one God resides
     in all.

(135)

O my soul, remember thy God;
thy years are rolling by without his sacred name.
Man without Harinama is even
like a well without water,
or a cow without milk,
or a temple without light,
or a fruit tree without fruit,
or body without eyes,
or night without the moon,
or the earth without rain,
or a pundit without a knowledge of the Vedas.
O good man, watch thy desire, anger, pride
and ambition and give them up.
Nanakshah says, O God
there is no one to befriend save thee.

(138)

Why hast thou given up Ramanama?
Thou hast not given up anger nor falsehood,
why hast thou given up truthful speech?
Being immersed in this false show
why hast thou abandoned the original home?
Thou hast treasured a cowrie,
why hast thou neglected the ruby?
Why hast thou given up remembering
that which is the source of all happiness?
Khalus says, Why wilt thou not trust God
and leave body, mind and wealth?

(139)

I have obtained a jewel in the shape of Ramanama.
The true guru gave me this priceless jewel
and showed his great favour to me.
I have obtained wealth for eternity;
what though I have lost everything of this earth?
This jewel cannot be used up by use, nor can it be
    stolen by thieves.
It increases greatly from day to day.
In the vessel called truth with the true guru as the captain
I have been able to cross the ocean of birth and death.
Mira says, I have sung the praise of the Lord in great
    glee.

(141)

For me there is none else but Giridhar Gopal,
let the whole world be witness.
I have given up brothers, friends, and other relatives.
In disregard of popular talk I sit in the midst of sadhus.
I rejoice to see God's devotees and weep to see worldly
    people.
I have reared the creeper of love with my tears.
I have churned the curds, extracted from them the
    butter
and thrown away the rest.
The King sent me a poison cup which I drank with
    pleasure.
Now does everybody know the story about me.
Mira says, Come what may,
I am intent upon God and God alone.

(144)

O my Ranaji, I must sing the praises of Govind.
If the King is angry he is welcome to his capital
but if God is angry where is one to flee?
Rana sent a poison cup,
I drank it as if it was nectar;
he sent a black snake in a box,
I took it for God Saligram.
Mirabai the love-stricken says,
I want Krishna as my Lord and Master.

(146)

O God, make me thy slave.

I shall be thy gardener and every day feast my eyes with
    the sight of thee.

I shall sing about the deeds of Govind in the groves and
    lanes of Brindaban.

For service I shall have daily *darshan,* and shall have as
    pocket money the memory of thee;

I shall get as estate intense devotion to thee; thus will I
    have the three excellent things.

My Lord has worn a peacock feather crown and a
    yellow *dhoti,*

he has worn a garland of *vaijanti* flowers,

he grazes cows in Brindaban and plays upon his pipe.

I shall build me a lofty palace and have windows in it;

through them I shall look at my Lord with my red sari
    on.

Among the inhabitants of Brindaban are to be found
    yogis doing yoga,

sannyasis doing *tapas,* sadhus singing *bhajans.*

Mira's Lord is deep and mysterious; keep thou thy
    patience—

He appears to his devotees even at midnight on the
    banks of the Jamuna.

(149)

One who speaks ill of me is a hero for me;
he works without pay.
He is instrumental in enabling me to wash off my old sins.
He renders me service without reward.
He sinks and saves others.
He is such a beloved fellow,
O Rama, I pray for his long life.
Dadu says, The vilifier is a benefactor in disguise.

(150)

O God,
Thou art sandal, I am as water;
thy sweet scent pervades everything.
Thou art the cloud, I am the peacock of the forest
looking for rain like the *chakor* bird for the moon;
thou art the lamp burning day and night, I am the wick;
thou art the pearl, I am the string,
and we unite as does gold with borax.
Ramdas the devotee says,
Thou art the Lord, I am the slave.

(152)

O God, my mind is distracted, how shall I worship
    thee?
Thou seest me, I should see thee, that were a sign of
    mutual love.
Thou seest me but I do not see thee, this is a state of a
    lost mind.
Though thou art in all always, yet have I not learnt to
    know thee!
Thou art full of virtue, I am full of vice.
I have not even acknowledged the debt owing to thee.
I am floundering between I and thou, thine and mine,
    how can I be saved?
Ramdas says, O God of mercy, hail to thee, the only
    stay of the universe.

(153)

A knowing man uses his knowledge at will.
Just as a vessel moving in all directions
is always guided by the polar star,
even so does the knowing one,
although moving about on earth,
have his gaze fixed on the heavens;
and just as the ice melts in water,
so does he attain his independence
by merging himself in the divine.
The condition is indescribable of him
whose abode is where the beginning
is unknown and the end never is,
and where neither the mind nor the speech can reach.
This divine play is wonderful and incomparable.
He who has known it from ancient times
speaks as it were from the heavens.
Akha says, Only a rare knowing one recognizes it.

(155)

In the world, the saints do the greatest good.
They lead us manifestly towards God and dispel our
     ignorance.
They are kind to all and, like God himself, assist us in
     our troubles.
They are above the three moods and have no thought
     of physical comforts.
They are different from the worldly men.
Brahmanand says, The company of saintly people
enables us to know God.

(160)

O thou, protector of the universe,
ruler of its destiny, abode of happiness and peace,
ocean of mercy, friend of the poor,
destroyer of the pangs of pauperism,
everlasting, whole, unending, beginningless,
perfect Brahma, ancient of days, refuge of the people,
their Lord, adored of them, matchless, indescribable,
beloved of the heart, guardian of the three worlds,
mainstay of life.

(162)

O God, my friend, I ask of thee this boon:
do not forget me.
I am dull-witted, know nothing,
nor do I show any love for thee.
Thou never forsakest those whom
thou hast taken under thy shelter;
thou wilt give me victory over thee.

I know that I have no merit
to commend itself to thee.
On the contrary, I have terrifying shortcomings
and, O my life, if thou, knowing my shortcomings,
wouldst give me up, I shall be undone.

But I have a certain faith in me
that thou wouldst not forsake me.
It is thy habit of old that thou ignorest
thy devotee's blemishes.
Thou art the friend of the poor,
thou art gentle of nature.
I adore thee.

Premsakhi says, I do not know thy mysteries,
only I believe in thee.

(164)

O beloved, I seek refuge in thee.
I have neither means nor strength, nor wisdom.
My sole faith is in the touch of thy feet, O Lord.
I am like the bitter fruit of low-lying ground,
but thou, ocean of mercy, has raised me high.
I am but a poor child seeking thy protection.
O Lord do not forget me who am so helpless.
O beloved, keep thou me, believing me to be thy slave.
Premsakhi says, I ever stake my all on thee.

(165)

O divine spirit, let me have a sight of thee.
By it I shall attain supreme bliss,
by it shall the endless chain of birth and death be
    broken.
For thee I have resorted to austerities,
penance and many ceremonies.
How long am I to continue?
Without thee all these are useless,
for the heart does not melt.
Some foolish ones hug action, others knowledge.
The joy and the value of union with thee
neither of them knows.
Thou art above them.
Thou art and art not in all.
In thy perfection thou art unique.
Thy action is a mystery.
Thou art both master and disciple.
Though formless and indescribable,
yet thou art all forms.
Thou alone knowest thyself.
The Vedas declare thee to be unknowable.
Thy servants sing thy praises.

(167)

I have now become immortal, I shall not die.
Why should I have to put on a new body
when I have given up self-deception, which is its cause?
Desire and anger bind one in the world.
These I shall destroy.
From time immemorial, man has died,
now I shall destroy time itself.
Body is mortal, soul is immortal;
it would revert to its original state.
I shall do away with the mortal
and become an inmate of the abode of the immortal.
I shall cleanse myself and be pure.
I have died many times because of my ignorance;
now I shall be free from the pair of happiness and
        unhappiness.
Anandghan says, Those who will not take shelter
under the two-lettered name that is so near everyone
will surely die.

(168)

All is Brahman.
Call it Rama or Rahman,
Kanha or Mahadev,
Parasnath or Brahma.

Pots are different but as earth they are one.
Even so do we make imaginary differentiations;
in essence, truth is one and indivisible.

He who is restraint incarnate is Rama,
he who is mercy incarnate is Rahim,
he who puts an end to all work by renouncing fruits is
     Kanha,
he who attains nirvana is Mahadev,
he who touches reality is Parasnath,
he who knows himself is Brahman.

Thus, says Anandghan,
I am spirit, not body, and am still.

(169)

My reliance is on the celebrated promise of God.
O God, my master, I know nothing of service or
    Ramanama.
Thou hast saved the elephant, the vulture, the prostitute
and the sinner Ajamil. I have sought thy protection
on the strength of this evidence of thy mercy.
Premanand says: O all-powerful and all-knowing Lord,
save me or kill me.

(171)

If thou wouldst see him, with each breath think of
    him.
Burn thy pride and smear thy body with its ashes;
take up the broom of love and with it wipe out the
    distinctions of me and thee;
reduce the notion of reality to dust and sprinkle it on
    thy prayer carpet;
leave the carpet, break up the rosary, throw the sacred
    books in the river,
seek the help of angels and be their servant;
do not fast nor keep *ramzan*,
do not go to the mosque nor make obeisances;
break to pieces the water jar for prayer cleansing
and drink the wine of the joy of union;
eat and drink but never be off thy guard;
enjoy thy intoxication continuously; burn thy egotism;
be neither mulla nor brahmin;
leave duality and worship him alone.
Shah Kalandar has proclaimed: Say, I am he.
Mad Mansur says, My heart has known truth.
That is the wine shop of the intoxicated.
Make that the object of thy visit.

(172)

Life in this world called beautiful garden
is only for a short while;
you will enjoy the spectacle for a few days only.
O traveller, prepare for the march;
residence on earth is short.

When the great hakim Lukman was asked,
"How long will you live?"
rubbing his hands in despair he replied,
"Only a few days."
After burial the angel of death said in the grave,
"You will sleep here only for a few days."
O friends, you and I will have to separate in a few days.
O tyrants, why do you oppress innocent people?
Your days are numbered.
Nazir says, Remember the day of death.
You cannot rely upon life but for a short while.

(173)

Note: Gandhi once supported a plan to sing one Muslim hymn
on a fixed day each week during prayers. He suggested that this
be the hymn. "We have been singing it from our days in South
Africa. It was introduced there by a pure-hearted Muslim youth.
That youth then passed away, so that for us the song has more in
it than its literal meaning. The song was so dear to that youth
that when he came to the line, 'Nazir, remember the day of death,'
he used to substitute his name, Hasan, for Nazir's." M.K.G.

Yes, now thou art the only King of my heart;
thou art my only beloved.
O creator, now my meditation is solely upon
thy sacred feet day and night.
My heart receives consolation only from thee;
thy love possesses me.
People generally consider me to be mad.
Everywhere thy name is on my tongue.
I have nothing to do with the pleasures of the world;
thy love is the only thing to please me.
My heart's case I shall paint with thy love.
Knowledge has united me to thee.
The prayer of thy servant is
that I may have nothing to do with Satan.

(174)

O God, thy law is mysterious.
Wherever the heart is set, there thou art to be seen;
with thee there is neither temple nor mosque.
Thou lookest only for a true heart in thy seeker.
Thou exhibitest the splendour of thy love
to him who has surrendered himself heart and soul to
     thee.
He who becomes enamoured of thy divine qualities
takes all his colouring from thee.
He in whom there is still egotism left
is like one who has lost his way,
and he is united to thee who has lost his egotism.
He who believes in thee sees thee face to face.
It is like a beggar finding a priceless pearl.

(175)

My boat is tiny and is laden with stones.
Eddies are tossing it from all sides
and the helmsman is drunk
and the boat is in midstream.
There is a whirlwind, and on the top of it all
rain is pouring in torrents.
Giridhar the poet says,
O Lord be thou the helmsman.
Let thy mercy be the oar,
and let the boat reach the shore safe.

(176)

O good woman, put on thy best garments;
thou art to go to thy Lord.
There the shroud will be of earth,
the bed will be of earth
and thou wilt be united to earth.
Wash, bathe, dress thy hair;
there is no returning from there.

(177)

He is a Vaishnava
who identifies himself with others' sorrows
and in so doing has no pride about him.
Such a one respects every one and speaks ill of none.
He controls his speech, his passions and his thoughts;
May his mother be blessed.
He is equidisposed towards all, has no desires,
regards another's wife as his mother,
always speaks the truth,
and does not touch other people's property.
He labours neither under infatuation nor delusion,
and withdraws his mind from worldly things.
He is intent on Ramanama,
his body is his sacred shrine for pilgrimage,
he is no miser and is free from cunning,
and he has conquered passions and anger.
Narasaiyo says,
His presence purifies his surroundings.

(178)

Note: Mahadev Desai, Gandhi's personal secretary, wrote that
this hymn "is almost as life-breath to Gandhiji and is sung on all
occasions when we are called upon to face sorrow and joy with
equanimity." It was sung as Gandhi ended his twenty-one day
fast for Hindu-Moslem friendship in October, 1924.

Know him to be a true man
who takes to his bosom those who are in distress.
Know that God resides in the heart of such a one.
His heart is saturated with gentleness through and
      through.
He receives as his only those who are forsaken.
He bestows on his man servants and maid servants
the same affection he shows to his children.
Tukaram says, What need is there to describe him
      further?
He is the very incarnation of divinity.

(179)

What can *maya* do to one who always remembers
     God?
By listening to God's word, by laying it to heart
and by meditating on man's oneness with God,
death ceases to frighten one.
The great God who is a fount of mercy and
giver of boons blesses such a one.
Amrit says, I therefore drink in nectar
by always contemplating Odhav's feet.

(183)

Give thyself to devotion and merge thyself in God.
Let people say what they like; for this,
thou shouldst store up overwhelming love.
Be indifferent to praise or blame,
leave off "me and thee," give up all desire
and devote thyself to desireless worship,
abandon all vain imaginings and doubts;
old age has crept over thee.
Man's estate is difficult to reach,
it will not come again for ages.
Having understood this, seek out a teacher.
Shivdini has no other determination.
He has given himself body and soul
to his teacher Kesarinath;
for him the world has ceased to exist.
Worship now God, the friend of his devotees.

(185)

Who will lay by stores that are bound to perish?
Why should one build houses, verandahs and storeys?
The humble cottage is good enough;
covering made of tattered rags is also good enough.
I should eat with relish whatever it pleases God
to give me from day to day.
Amrit says, What is filled in the beggar's bowl
gives all the relish one wants—it is such a joy.

(186)

If thou wouldst be a yogi, thou must attend to the necessary observances. Know that he who is slave to his tongue and sold himself to the goddess of sleep will never practise yoga. The candidate for yoga should be moderate in sleep and food, and must not indulge in vain disputations.

Make up thy mind thus to regulate thy food and all thy movements, practise internal concentration, and then thou wouldst have internal peace. When thy mind is taken off external objects it will easily turn inward and be fixed, even as a light protected from winds becomes steady and fixed.

(189)

Wherever I go, thou art my companion.
Having taken me by the hand thou movest me.
I go alone depending solely on thee.
Thou bearest too my burdens.
If I am likely to say anything foolish, thou makest it right.
Thou hast removed my bashfulness and madest me
self-confident.
O Lord, all the people have become my guards, relatives
and bosom friends.
Tuka says, I now conduct myself without any care.
I have attained divine peace within and without.

(190)

To the servants of Vishnu
there is no yearning even for salvation,
they do not want to know
what the wheel of birth and death is like,
Govind sits steadily settled in their hearts,
for them the beginning and the end are the same.
They make over happiness and misery to God
and themselves remain untouched by them,
the auspicious songs sing of them,
their strength and their intellect are dedicated to
    benevolent uses,
their hearts contain gentleness,
they are full of mercy even like God,
they know no distinction between theirs and others'.
Tuka says, They are even like unto God,
and Vaikuntha is where they live.

(192)

Saintliness is not to be purchased in shops,
nor is it to be had for wandering,
nor in cupboards nor in deserts nor in forests.
It is not obtainable for a heap of riches.
It is not in the heavens above, nor in the entrails of the
    earth below.
Tuka says, It is a life's bargain
and if you will not give your life to possess it
better be silent.

(194)

Merit consists in doing good to others,
sin in doing harm to others.
There is no other pair comparable to this.
Truth is the only religion,
untruth is bondage.
There is no secret like this.
God's name on one's lips is itself salvation,
disregard of the name know to be perdition.
Companionship of the good is the only heaven,
studious indifference is hell.
Tuka says, It is thus clear what is good and what is
    injurious,
let people choose what they will.

(201)

O God, grant only this boon;
I may never forget thee, and I shall prize it dearly.
I desire neither salvation nor riches nor prosperity.
Give me always company of the good.
Tuka says, On that condition
thou mayest send me to the earth again and again.

(203)

O thou dweller in my heart,
open it out, purify it, make it bright and beautiful,
awaken it, prepare it, make it fearless,
make it a blessing to others,
rid it of laziness, free it from doubt,
unite it with all, destroy its bondage,
let thy peaceful music pervade all it works.
Make my heart fixed on thy holy lotus feet
and make it full of joy, full of joy, full of joy.

(204)

Endless stream of joy flows eternally,
ancient music sounds in the boundless sky,
innumerable suns, moons and stars rise.
That matchless King of Kings shines
in all his glory in the whole universe.
Ten million hearts of devotees,
astonished, motionless, speechless,
bow their heads before the feet of the almighty.

(205)

O good man, remember God and give up thy egotism,
think of the source from which thou hast come.
What art thou and what dost thou cling to?
Without understanding the root of things
thou sayst, "This is mine, that is mine."
But if thou wilt use thy judgment thou wilt observe
that the body is not thine, for try what thou wilt,
thou canst not keep it for ever, it is bound to perish.
When this body perishes there will be many more new
    ones
and thy wife, children and others will deceive thee.
Thou thinkest always of wealth
and that is the greatest stumbling block in thy way.
Thy lord is near thee and thou dost not know him,
thou hast lost thy chance and wasted thy time.
Thou art in deep sleep and suffocated.
Why wilt thou not listen to the words of the sages and
    wake up?
Narsaiyo says, It is a matter of shame thou wilt not
    wake up.
If thou only wilt, thy age-long desires will abate.

(210)

Throughout the whole universe thou alone art,
thou appearest as many, taking diverse forms,
thou art the informing being in the material body,
thou art the essence of light,
thou art the word of the Vedas in the void,
thou art the air, water, earth.
O Lord, thou spreadest out high up in the trees,
similarly having created a multitude of forms and a
    variety of tastes.
From one being thou hast become many.
The Vedas declare and the other shastras bear witness
that there is no distinction between a nugget of gold
and a gold ear-ring; when it undergoes shapes, it wears
different appearances and different names but in reality
    it is all gold.
Thou art the seed in the tree and thou art the tree from
    the seed,
and from this phenomenon one sees change in form.
Narsaiyo says, This is all a matter of the mind,
but if I worship thee in true faith, thou wilt appear as
    thou art.

(211)

As long as the secret of the soul is not known,
all practices are useless;
thy life as a human being has passed away
uselessly, like the rains out of season.
What though thou bathest daily and performest
worship and dost service in the temples,
what though thou givest alms staying in thy own house,
what though thou adoptest long hair,
smearest thy body with the sacred ashes,
What though thou hast removed thy hair,
performest austerities and visitest holy places,
what though thou takest the rosary and takest his name;
what though thou markest the sacred mark
on the forehead, and keepest the tulsi leaf,
what though thou drinkest the Ganges water;
what though thou can recite the Vedas
and knowest the grammar and pronouncest correctly,
what though thou knowest the tunes and their effect,
what though thou knowest the six systems
and the permutations and combinations of letters.
All these are devices for finding
the wherewithal for one's support
if thou hast not known the soul of souls.
Narsaiyo says,
Thou hast wasted the priceless human heritage
if thou hast not known the secret of the universe.

(212)

O dear Lord, I love thy face;
as soon as I saw thy face, the world became useless to me
and my mind became detached from it.
The happiness that the world gives is like a mirage;
one should move about deeming it of no account.
Mirabai says, blessed Lord, my only hope is in thee,
and I consider myself fortunate in that I have seen thee
    face to face.

(219)

Thou hast not yet become a devotee of God;
what is thy pride based on?
Thy heart does not swell with joy to see men of God,
it does not melt to sing God's praises.
Thy desires have not abated,
thy eyes are red with anger.
Thou wilt be a true Vaishnava
if thou canst draw another towards thee.
Thou art nothing so long as thy contact
does not influence one for the better,
thou art not pained to see others in pain,
thou dost not hesitate to speak ill of others,
thou hast no true love for God,
thou art not ashamed of repeating "I, I."
Thou hast no liking for serving others,
thou canst not give up selfishness,
thy acts don't accord with thy speech,
when challenged thou deniest thy speech,
thou hast no relish for prayer,
thou hast no faith in God.
So long as thou hankerest after the world,
the world is thy master and thou its slave.
If thou wilt master thyself thou wilt find the true thing.
Daya says, Whether thou likest it or not,
I must say what is true.

(220)

O God, such as I am, I am thy servant.
O ocean of mercy, take me by the hand,
thou art companion in distress
thou art protector of the fallen,
thou dost not dismiss from thy presence
the wretch who seeks thy protection
no matter how much sunk he may be in sin.
O thou deliverer, thou shieldest thy devotees
who may be tempted to do wrong,
thou givest fortune to the unfortunate and
O giver of boons, thou givest capacity and satisfaction.
O good Lord, thou makest crooked straight
even when human endeavour has failed.
O God who deliverest from misery,
thou washest the sins of the undeserving sinner,
thou protectest thy devotees without their asking,
thou reckonest their faults as merit,
thou removest the difficulties of those who invoke thy
    aid,
thou dost not distinguish between the great and the
    small,
thou art the help of the helpless,
thou knowest the aches of men's hearts,
thou art the friend of the afflicted,
thou sufferest,
thou takest away fear from men
and thou overlookest blemishes.

thou art the Lord of all, the soul of souls,
thou alone art independent,
thou art the beloved of Pritam,
thou art the guardian of thy servants.
Thou art my rock.

(221)

Godward way is for the brave not for the cowardly.
Before one can treasure the sacred name in the heart,
it is necessary to be ready to lay down one's life.
He only gets that divine joy
who surrenders children, wife, wealth and his own head.
Those who would find pearls
risk their lives in going in deep waters;
such people face death bravely
and have no doubts lurking in their minds.
But those who watch these brave deeds from a safe
    distance
shiver even to think of the risks.
The way of love is a fiery ordeal, cowards flee before it.
Those who are in it enjoy rare happiness,
the spectators are scorched.
Love is a bargain of life not to be easily had.
Those who have attained the heights
have passed through the fire of self-purification.
Those who have drunk deep of the nectar
of Ramanama are an object of envy.
But those only who know what divine love is
recognize them when they see them.
They witness the divine sport of Pritam's Lord.

(224)

No matter what one does,
self-denial will not last unless it is based
on dislike for the thing given up.
If there is deep down the desire for it,
it will not be relinquished.
A man may wear the garb of a *sannyasi*
but that will bring him no nearer the goal
if the garb only hides the desire
that has its full possession of the wearer.
So long as desire, anger, greed and passion
are not rooted out, the thing will come to the surface
the moment there is an opportunity;
the very *sannyasa* may become
an additional source of self-indulgence.
Just as the seed does not sprout during
the dry hot season, but does so as soon
as the rains come, so is it with man's desires—
they await the due season.
Just as iron moves in front of a magnet,
so do the senses move when they are
face to face with their objects.
They are still for want of opportunity,
but they run riot as soon as the opportunity comes.
Therefore mere external renunciation will not answer
if there is no corresponding response within.
Such external renunciation will mean licence
even from the restraints of Varnashrama,

the four divisions, and is likely to result in harm.
Such a man becomes useless like milk gone bad.
It won't yield ghee or butter and is unfit to drink.
Nishkulanand says, A man's renunciation is wrong
when he hovers between self-denial and self-indulgence,
household affairs and their relinquishment.

(226)

The yogi has migrated to the forest.
He has given up all love of the body,
he cares not to talk about the world,
he has become indifferent about its comforts.
He who had richly upholstered cots
and lived in palaces has not even straw to lie on,
lives in the shade of trees.
He who had rich shawls and embroidered robes
now sports a ragged blanket and bears heat and cold.
He who had a variety of tasty foods
now lives upon pieces of chapati
thrown in the begging bowl.
He at whose call thousands answered
and who was followed by large armies
is now wandering, alone and unshod.

O King, if you would stop I would prepare food for you.
I would prepare rice puddings in no time
and it will be put in your begging bowl.

The King answers:
He who waits for food, expects to have a dish, is no yogi,
he is a householder desirous of enjoyment.
He is doomed.
He who gives up his kingdom and adopts *sannyasa*
may not fix his mind on wealth and family,
he considers all indulgence as a malady.

Nishkulanand says, Blessed be he
who gives up all desire for physical comforts
and adopts *sannyasa*,
he has left his family, it is true,
but he has gained an imperishable family.

(227)

They are patient and brave and true warriors
who have shed all fear of death.
Even if there are tens of millions against one
they will regard them as straw.
They have to face the determined enemy called
     temptation,
but they will not flinch even though they should die.
Poets, noted pundits, are very intellectual,
but they would not face such an enemy—
for in that army desire, anger, vanity, ambition are chief
     warriors.
For the learned, there is no standing against this army.
Wandering yogis, ascetics and the like
fight under the shelter of God.
Against such an army true warriors alone fight.
Yogis know through the mouths of their teachers the
     art of fighting.
Muktanand says, After having defeated this army
of temptations they enjoy immortal bliss.

(229)

Those who will not break their plighted word are real
     heroes.
They will not be moved from their purpose by any of
     the three fevers,
they will act with decision and patience,
they would never harbour doubt about their action or
     its timeliness.
We have to die some day without fail, some sooner,
     some later.
Let us not flinch for the sake of worldly enjoyment.
He who understands things clearly through the heart
and then acts in the teeth of all danger is a hero.
He will not entertain suspicions about others,
he will never forget Brahmanand's God.

(230)

We must risk life itself but realize God,
we may never recede from the attempt.
I looked within . . . and placed my head at the feet of
    Hari.
One may not move without knowing
the wisdom of the step, but having moved forward
there should be no looking back;
in the field of strife we must fight unto death.
With what face can one return who bravely
goes forward and then at the critical moment
beats a hasty retreat?
It is wise to make calculations beforehand;
it is no use going out to battle in bravado.
But having once gone, there should be no retiring
even though one may be cut to pieces.
We must sing of Hari with zest
and may not step back when the call comes.
Brahmanand says, We should rather die than accept
    defeat.

(231)

My pulse is in thy hands, O God.
Take care of me, regarding me as thine.
Keep thy prestige.

I do not know what is good for me and what is not,
misery always stares me in the face.
O God, look at me, what is happening to me?
Thou art the true physician from time immemorial;
thou knowest all the remedies.
My time is near, do thou be punctual.
O God, why art thou waiting?
Why dost thou give me up whilst there is yet hope ?
O God, do thou remove my great misery.

Keshav says, What will happen to me?
I am undone if the whole battle is lost.
Be thou warned, O my protector,
thy prestige will be lost if anything happens to thy
    servant.

(233)

O lord of the afflicted, do not desert me.
In this great ocean of birth and death I am tossed about;
do not let the occasion of saving me slip by.
Thou art my only refuge, I do not know the means.
O keeper of my life, do not give me up because I am so
    worthless;
thou art mother, father, family, all in all.
O ocean of mercy, do not dry up for thy slave's sake.
Keshavlal has thy protection;
O lord of the universe, desert me not on any account.

(234)

The mountain is in the straw but no one sees it there
even as none would notice a lion hidden among a flock
   of sheep.
But he can discover himself by his roar,
as the musk deer among the ordinary flock.
The absolute is hidden in the phenomenal
as oil in the seed, fire in the wood, ghee in milk.
Who will listen and to whom shall I talk
of the illimitable and the unknowable?
Speech does not reach it.
There is an abode which is beyond the intellect.
Though the mind is swift like the wind it cannot
   overtake it.
This immortal, indivisible essence
pervades everything movable and immovable.
It has made this universe,
there is not an atom where it is not,
but by the grace of a true guru it is attainable.
Why go in search of it here and there when it is in you?
Servant Dhiro says, Thou art wherever I look.

(239)

Resolve upon enthroning Ramanama in thy heart.
Yoga is no use, nor is the saffron-coloured robe
nor mixing up all thy food.
Whether thou wearest *bhagava* or white garments
is of little consequence.
The thing to do is not to hurt any creature
and to wish it well.
Put the worldly men on one side, the yogis on the other
and then show me the yogi who has seen God face to face.
Because they served God,
Narasinha Mehta, Mira, Prahlad, Sena barber,
Dhano, Peepo, Rohidas, Koobo, Potter Goro,
Rajput Bodano, Gangabai saw God face to face.
Poor good people, good-hearted butchers,
worshipped God and found peace;
show me the yogi who did likewise.
Rama is not to be attained by smearing oneself with ashes,
nor by hanging head downward,
nor by leaving wife and retiring to the forest.
God can be attained only by diligent search.
Rama is for him who can be happy in the jungle
and who regards palaces as jungle,
who regards bitter as sweet and sweet like bitter.
Even as oil is hid in the seed, ghee in milk,
so is God hid everywhere, says Narbho.

(242)

Men of God should have abundant love for all;
they should shed all egotism.
Through God's name they should
banish the threefold afflictions,
leave off sinning and take Ramanama.
They should consider all to be good
and themselves to be unworthy.
They should in perfect humility distribute alms.
They should devote themselves to
their faith, body, mind and speech,
and regard God as the giver and the enjoyer.
They should not weaken in their decisions;
they should speak sparingly.
They should entrust secrets only to the trustworthy
and their speech should be humble
and they should be serious in giving opinions;
they must not talk big before those who know how to
        discriminate.
They should take the name of the limitless God
and attain salvation, and help others to do likewise.
Their devotion should be as of poor people.
Bhojo, a humble servant, says, By the grace of God
the three afflictions do not go near such people.

(243)

Devotion is for the brave,
they do not turn back after having once begun.
Having made up their minds, they go forward in full faith.
They have killed desire, anger, arrogance and greed.
When the temptations swelled and when the heat
    commenced,
the cowards trembled and fled.
The true men stood their ground and fought
with God as their help and guide.
They outdistanced many and then began to have a
    glimpse of Brahman.
They destroyed the effect of past action and met God
    face to face.
They would not wish for the various gifts.
To such salvation is easy.
Bhojo Bhakta says,
Those who have given up themselves body and mind
    and all,
and are ever equi-minded,
are the true devotees,
and they have heaven as their abode.

(244)

O teacher, you say Brahman is in me but I see him
    not;
tell me what distinguishes him.
Is the head he or is the head in him,
is he in the eyes or are the eyes themselves Brahman ?
Is he in the nose or in the mouth?
I am puzzled. Pray help me out of my doubt and
    delusion.
Is he in the feet or in the hands, in the heart or the
    chest?
If he is in the feet, where is he?
O teacher, teach me.

When the pupil was rested, the teacher spoke:
O pupil, listen, today the ignorance must be dispelled.
He, the loved one, is not in any particular limb, let me
    warn you betimes,
He eludes one unless one enquires within.
He is as near as you are intent upon him.
Therefore when one is absorbed in him,
one sees him, though he has neither form nor colour.
Bapu says, Yet you will see him in many forms.

(245)

O tongue, why dost thou tire of singing God's praises?
Thou hast not enough time for gossip,
which is ever on thy lips.
Thou art expert in talking ill of others.
Thou art ever ready for tasty things;
thou art ready also for quarrelling.
But when it comes to the matter of
praising the Lord, thou art too busy.
At the time of death no one is of any use,
the dear ones are like so many foes. . . .
When the time approaches sesame is sent for
and so is tulsi leaf. Ramanama is also taken.
But when you were young
you carried yourself with a high head.
What is the use of Ramanama on the death-bed?
Is it any use digging a well after a house has caught fire?
Of what use is a light brought
after the thieves have stolen things?
You are intoxicated with your own infatuation;
wake up and look around.
What is the use of weeping when time knocks at the door?
It costs nothing to sing Hari's praises,
not a hair is touched.
The weary way will not be passed without effort,
but the whole can be easily covered by reliance upon God.

(246)

The works of him who has an inner experience
do not bind him, for he has known God.
He is the knowing one who has broken all ties.
He is beyond everything and is a mere witness of
    everything;
he is independent of all the six worlds.
Being above these he stands alone.
Of millions the fewest only realize this.
One who has the inner experience knows the nameless
    one.
He has attained salvation for he is past the dual state;
without striving for the one indivisible,
he perceives it as if naturally.
The truth is that all created things have to perish
and so this endless ocean of life and death continues to
    roll on.
The last stage is beyond waking, dreaming, sleeping
and the state beyond these three.
It is beyond the physical and ethereal.
That which is above even the first cause
is described by the Vedas as "not this, not this."
I dote on the mother of him who has dedicated himself
to common good, who is goodness personified
and who is like the true guru. Nirant says,
He who is eternal, though nameless, has many names.

(250)

Light thy heart and sweep out from there
evil thoughts and anger.
Let mercy be oil and love the oil tray,
let meditation on God be the wick
and let knowledge of Brahman be the light.
When the heart is thus truly lighted
all darkness will vanish
and then thou shalt recognize God's abode.
O men, recognize this light that dispels darkness.
Ranchhod says, I have entered the home,
have found the key and opened the lock,
and there is light on earth.

(251)

When will the matchless time come
so that I would be rid of all knots—external and
    internal?
When will I give up all the subtlest ties
and go the way the great sages have gone?
Would that I was indifferent to all the moods
and that the body was used merely for self-restraint,
that there was nothing to bind me
for any cause imaginable,
and that I had no illusions about the body.
Would that I should gain knowledge that comes
from removal of obstruction in the path of perception,
that I regarded body as separate from the soul,
and that I had recognition only of the soul.
Would that obstruction to right conduct, too,
was removed, and there was concentration on pure self.
Would that there was steadfastness of the three *yugas*
running practically to the time of death,
and that steadfastness was incapable of being shaken
by sufferings, however great.
Would that even yoga was only
for attaining greater restraint over self,
and that there was implicit obedience
to the precepts of the Jina for the sake of the soul.
Would that even that activity also perceptibly decreased,
and I was absorbed in self-realization.
Would that there were neither likes nor dislikes

in matters received through the senses,
and that I was unaffected by their play.
Would that I engaged in activities
that came to me in due course and was not enslaved
by time, place or circumstance.
Would that I was angered against anger
and that against respect paid to me I had
humility enough not to be affected by it.
Would that in respect of *maya*
I was but a witness to its blandishments,
and against ambition I had ambition to thwart it,
that I had no anger against even the extreme wrongdoer
and had no pride if an emperor paid respects to me,
that I was unmoved even if the body perished
and had no desire even for the greatest gifts,
that I was the same to friend and foe alike
as towards praise or insult,
that there was indifference in me whether I lived or died,
that even regarding the cycles of birth and death or
        salvation
I had only the simple natural state,
that I had crossed the alluring ocean of different
        temptations
and was intent upon the state where all passions are
        quenched,
that at the time of death
I would shed all desire and have perfect knowledge,
that all the four kinds of activities
were to me like a burnt hope—mere ashes,
that I was living out only this life

and that after that there was no more birth,
that I had no desire for even an atom,
that I was sinless, immovable and intent upon self-
    realization,
that I was absorbed in the spotless, eternal, everliving,
neither small nor big, formless, self-acting being,
that owing to past actions I was fit
for the abode of the released, where there is eternal bliss,
perfect perception and perfect experience.
This is the state which the all-knowing Jina
realized but could not describe.
How can any other person describe it?
It is capable only of being experienced.
I have set my heart upon that state
though it may be at present beyond my capacity.
Nevertheless Rajchand is determined
that, God willing, he will attain that state.

(252)

How neglectful must my eyes be
that they never saw Hari.
They never set their gaze upon him,
they would not be calm enough
even to have a glimpse of him.
They have been immersed in sorrows or enjoyments,
have burnt themselves with their heat.
They have not devoted themselves
to having God's *darshan,* and yet
God is everywhere, he fills his creation.
Among the movable and the immovable objects
there is not an atom but has his presence in it.
He is like the heavens pervading all.
He is like the air inhabiting my heart.
If I would but look at him,
he is there staring me in the face.
Brahma and his creation cannot be separated
even for a moment, but we of the earth earthy
have no inkling of that vital principle;
an owl may live for a hundred years
and still will not know what the day is like.
The Lord is like the ocean—
too big for the eyes to scan.
The tongue gets fatigued to tell of him
and so simply says he is vast.
O God, when will the spiritual sight be opened?
When will this deep darkness be dispelled?

O God, listen to my petition
and lift this dead curtain.
O my eyes, look deep and there is Hari.
O eyes, get rid of the laziness and calmly see him.
Just set the gaze upon him
and look at him to heart's content.

(253)

Appendix:
Two Christian Hymns

"When I Survey the Wondrous Cross" and "Pillar of the Cloud" were among Gandhi's favorite hymns. Because they were composed in English, these lyrics were not included in his translation of *Ashram Bhajanavali* for Mirabehn. A selection of Gandhi's ashram prayers would be incomplete without them.

When I survey the wondrous cross
on which the Prince of glory died,
my richest gain I count but loss,
and pour contempt on all my pride.

See, from his head, his hands, his feet,
sorrow and love flow mingled down.
Did e'er such love and sorrow meet?
or thorns compose so rich a crown?

Since I, who was undone and lost,
have pardon through his name and word;
forbid it, then, that I should boast,
save in the cross of Christ, my Lord.

Were the whole realm of nature mine,
that were a tribute far too small.
Love so amazing, so divine,
demands my life, my soul, my all.

Note: This lyric, written by Isaac Watts in 1707, is referred to
frequently in Gandhi's writings on prayer. It was sung in private
services, at Gandhi's request, as he ended rigorous fasts in 1924
and 1948.

Lead, kindly light, amid th'encircling gloom, lead thou
   me on!
The night is dark, and I am far from home; lead thou
   me on!
Keep thou my feet; I do not ask to see
the distant scene; one step enough for me.

I was not ever thus, nor prayed that thou shouldst lead
   me on;
I loved to choose and see my path; but now lead thou
   me on!
I loved the garish day, and, spite of fears,
pride ruled my will. Remember not past years!

So long thy power hath blessed me, sure it will, will
   lead me on.
o'er moor and fen, o'er crag and torrent, till the night is
   gone,

Note: This hymn, entitled, "Pillar of the Cloud," was written in
1833 by Cardinal John Henry Newman. It was often sung at
prayer meetings in a Gujarati translation, *Premal Jyoti.* In 1932,
Father Verrier Elwin, an English admirer, proposed to Gandhi
that he sing a Christian hymn at an appointed hour each week, so
that others might "mentally be in communion" with him. This hymn
was selected accordingly, and sung each Friday at 7:30 P.M. by
friends in America, Europe, India, and other countries.

and with the morn those angel faces smile,
which I have loved long since, and lost awhile!

Meantime, along the narrow rugged path, thyself hast
    trod,
lead, Savior, lead me home in child-like faith, home to
    my God,
to rest forever after earthly strife
in the calm light of everlasting life.

Index of First Lines

Just as rivers rushing towards the sea 40
Know him to be a true man 99
Lead, kindly light, amid th'encircling gloom 144
Let him be whosoever he may be 35
Life in this world called beautiful garden 93
Light thy heart and sweep out from there 135
Listen to the essence of religion 48
May the goddess of learning, Saraswati 31
May the winds, the waters, the plant life 42
Men of God should have abundant love for all 130
Merit consists in doing good to others 107
My boat is tiny and is laden with stones 96
My pulse is in thy hands, O God 126
My reliance is on the celebrated promise of God 91
No matter what one does, self-denial will not last 119
O beloved, I seek refuge in thee 87
O dear Lord, I love thy face 114
O divine spirit, let me have a sight of thee 88
O father, I will not give up Ramanama 70
O friend, my mind is fixed on a fakir's life 67
O God, ever since I have had the companionship 73
O God, grant only this boon 108
O God, I seek refuge in thee 72
O God, make me thy slave 79
O God, my friend, I ask of thee this boon 86
O God, my mind is distracted, how shall I worship 82
O God, such as I am, I am thy servant 116
O God, thou art sandal 81
O God, thy law is mysterious 95
O good man, natural meditation is best 65
O good man, remember God and give up thy egotism 111
O good woman, put on thy best garments 97
O Gopal, I have danced away my life 62
O lord of the afflicted, do not desert me 127
O Lord! Hear this my prayer 54

O Mukunda! With head bowed down I ask of thee 49
O, my heart 50
O my Ranaji, I must sing the praises of Govind 78
O my soul, remember thy God 74
O Prince of the Raghus, wake up 57
O Raghuvir, help of the distressed 55
O teacher, you say Brahman is in me but I see him not 132
O thou dweller in my heart 109
O thou, protector of the universe 85
O tongue, why dost thou tire of singing God's praises 133
O! goddess Earth 30
Om! May God protect us 44
Om! From untruth lead me unto truth 45
One may not abandon one's faith 43
One who speaks ill of me is a hero for me 80
Open thy face, thou wilt see thy beloved 64
Regard the soul as the warrior, body as his chariot 37
Resolve upon enthroning Ramanama in thy heart 129
Saintliness is not to be purchased in shops 106
Self-realization comes always through truth 39
Soul-force is superior even to science 41
That which goes by the name of adversity is not such 34
The mountain is in the straw but no one sees it 128
The works of him who has an inner experience 134
The yogi has migrated to the forest 121
They are patient and brave and true warriors 123
Those knowing ones who, with austerities and faith 36
Those who will not break their plighted word 124
Thou art merciful, I am in distress 52
Thou hast not yet become a devotee of God 115
Throughout the whole universe thou alone art 112
To the servants of Vishnu 105
We are not to stay here long 66
We must risk life itself but realize God 125
What can maya do to one who always remembers God? 100

Glossary

Ahimsa—Non-violence.

Akha (1600-1655)—Gujarati philosopher poet.

Anandghan—Seventeenth-century Gujarati poet. Sadhu of the Jain religion.

Bali—A powerful king of the Daityas in an age when these beings were attacking the gods. Vishnu descended as a divine Dwarf and in three steps expanded to cosmic size, sending Bali to the underworld.

bhagava—Saffron; refers to the saffron-colored robe of an ascetic.

bhajans—Devotional songs.

Bhojo (1785-1750)—Gujarati metaphysical poet.

Bhojo Bhakta—Bhojo.

Brahma—The Creator God, often mentioned along with Vishnu and Shiva as the supreme triad of gods.

Brahman—The supreme Godhead; ultimate reality.

Brahmanand (1772-1849)—Gujarati renunciant and saint-poet.

Brahmin—Member of the Hindu priestly caste.

Brindaban—The forest around the village where Krishna spent his childhood and youth; scene of his cowherding, playing with friends, and nocturnal trysts.

Dadu (1544-1603)— Saint-poet; a low-caste cotton-carder in whose name an important sectarian movement, the Dadu Panth, was formed.

darshan—Viewing; the religiously charged act of seeing a sacred representation of a deity, a holy person or place.

Dasharatha—The father of Rama.

Daya (1777-1853)—Gujarati devotional poet.

dharma—Law, duty; the universal law.

Dhiro (1753-1825)—Gujarati philosophical poet.

dhoti—A cloth wrapped around the lower body and worn as a garment.

Draupadi—Wife of the Pandavas, five brothers who are the heroes of the Mahabharata.

Dushasana—Royal enemy of the Pandus in the Mahabarata, who attempts to strip off Draupadi's sari in the royal assembly. Krishna miraculously saves Draupadi.

fakir—Muslim ascetic, often a wonder worker.

Four Divisions—The four castes of Indian Hindu society: Brahmin (priestly); Kshatriya (warrior); Vaisya (merchants and farmers); Sudra (servants).

Giridhar—"Lifter of Mountain"; epithet of Krishna.

Gopal—"Cowherd"; an epithet of Krishna.

Govind—"Cow finder"; an epithet for Krishna.

Hari—"One who takes possission of"; epithet of Vishnu,

Harinama—"Hari's name," referring to the religious power of repeating God's name.

Indra—A sky god; king of the gods in the Vedic pantheon.

Jamuna—River in the region of Brindaban, where the young Krishna lived.

Jina—An enlightened person (lit. "conqueror"), in the Jain religion.

Kabir—Fifteenth century Indian weaver and mystical poet. Muslim by birth, he honored the universal in all religions and criticized religious hypocrisy and arrogance.

Kaliyuga—The Age of Kali, last of four ages in the repeating cycles of time; the present age, a time marked by stife and dissension.

Kanha—epithet of Krishna

Keshav (1524-1571)—Marathi saint-poet.

Krishna—An incarnation of Vishnu.

Lotus-eyed One—Epithet used for many gods. In prayer 75 probably refers to Vishnu.

Mahadev—"The Great God", often an epithet of Siva.

Mahavir—Sixth-century B.C. enlightened being; the historical founder of Jainism.

Mandir—Temple.

Manu—Legendary person believed to have composed (perhaps c. 300) the Laws of Manu, an important treatise on social organization and customs.

maya—Illusion; the manifest world.

Mira—Mirabai.

Mirabai (1498-1565)—Rajasthani princess, devotee of Krishna. Upon the death of her husband she escaped murder at the hands of Rana, the king, and became a wandering ecstastic poet. Songs attributed to her are in Gujarati, Hindi and Rajasthani.

Muktanand (1761-1830)—Gujarati poet and monk.

Mukunda—"The Deliverer", an epithet of Vishnu.

Mulla—Muslim ritual specialist.

Nanak (1469-1538)—Founder of the Sikh religion. Mystic poet whose compositions are in Punjabi.

Nanakshah—Nanak.

Nandalal—Epithet of Krishna.

Narasaiyo (b. 1414)—Narasimha Mehta, wandering mystic poet and devotee of Krishna. Regarded as "The Father of Gujarati Poetry."

Narasimha—Incarnation of Vishnu, half man-lion, who saved Prahlad by killing Hiranyakashipu.

Nirant (1770-1846)—Gujarati poet.

Nirvana—Extinction of self-will, realization of the absolute.

Odhav—Teacher of the poet Amrit.

Om—The sacred syllable, believed to be the sound of ultimate reality.

Parasnath—Believed to be the first Jina, liberated teacher, in the Jain tradition.

Prahlad—Devout son of the demon Hiranyakashipu, who was saved by Vishnu.

Premanand—(1779-1845)—Gujarati poet.

Premsakhi—"A female friend," used by Premanand in addressing Krishna and his guru.

Pritam (1720-1798)—Gujarati monk and poet.

Puranas—Ancient Hindu myths and legends

Purushottama—Epithet of Rama

Putna—"Stinking"; a demoness who attempts to kill the baby Krishna by giving him her poisoned breast.

Raghus—The descendants of Raghu, great-grandfather of Rama.

Raghuvir—"Raghu hero"; epithet of Ram.

Rahim—Muslim name for God

Rahman—Muslim name for God

Rajchand (1867-1901)—Poet and businessman, friend of Gandhi, devout follower of Jainism.

Rama—An incarnation of Vishnu; hero of the Ramayana.

Ramanama—"Rama's name," referring to the religious power of repeating God's name.

Ramdas—Seventeenth-century poet and devotee of Rama. Author of the *Dasabodha*.

ramzan—Ramadan, the month of fasting during daylight hours that Muslims practice every year.

Ranchhod—Eighteenth-century Gujarati devotional poet.

sadhus—Renunciants or holy men.

Saligram—A round stone with distinctive marks, believed to be an embodiment of Vishnu.

sannyasa—Vows of renunciation

sannyasi—A person who gives up all possessions and family to devote life to the pursuit of God.

Shankara—Eighth-century philosopher and guru, founder of Advaita Vedanta, which rejects dualism; also "Bringing about eternal welfare", an epithet of Siva.

shanti—Perfect inner peace.

shastras—Treatises on Hindu religious and social custom, which include the Laws of Manu.

Shrikrishna—Krishna (Shri = honorific term).

Siva—One of the great gods of Hinduism, worshiped as supreme by many, known as the cosmic dancer who dances the universe in and out of existence.

Sudama—A childhood friend of Krishna who, as a very poor and humble adult, goes to see Krishna in the splendor of his royal court. Krishna blesses him with great prosperity.

Surdas (1478-1563)—Mystical Indian poet, devotee of Krishna, traditionally understood to be blind.

tapas—Lit. "heat"; self-control; spiritual power acquired through austerity.

Tuka—Tukaram

Tukaram (1598-1649)—Devotional Marathi poet who wrote of the power of God's grace.

Tulsi—Tulsidas; also, a plant (a variety of basil) sacred to Vishnu.

Tulsidas (d. 1623)—Mystical poet, author of the popular and revered Hindi devotional version of the Ramayana epic.

Vaikuntha—Paradise; the abode of Vishnu.

Vaishnava—Devotee of Vishnu.

Valmiki—Author to whom the Sanskrit Ramayana, the epic of Rama (probably c. 200 B.C.) is attributed.

Varnashrama—A brahminical ideal of dharma that includes living appropriately according to one's social class *(varna)* and stage of life *(ashrama)*.

Vedas—Sacred hymn collections of the ancient Indo-Aryans.

Veena— A traditional Indian stringed instrument.

Vishnu—One of the great gods of Hinduism, worshiped as supreme by many; Known for his series of avatars in which he descends to save the earth from the forces of evil.

Yuga—An age. In the tradition described by the Indian epics, there are four successive yugas, which degenerate in length and moral quality. At the end of these, the universe dissolves and the cycle begins again. The present yuga is the fourth, the Kaliyuga.

Contributors

ARUN GANDHI is the fifth grandson of Mahatma Gandhi. Raised in South Africa at the Phoenix Ashram, a religious community established by his grandfather in 1904, he moved to India as a teenager in 1945, and lived with the Mahatma during the last years of his life. Dr. Gandhi is a former journalist, and with his wife, Sunanda, started India's Center for Social Unity, an organization dedicated to alleviating poverty and caste discrimination. The author of eight books, Dr. Gandhi has been a resident of the United States since 1987. He and his wife are founders of the M. K. Gandhi Institute for Nonviolence at Christian Brothers University in Memphis, Tennessee.

MICHAEL NAGLER is Professor Emeritus of Classics and Comparative Literature at the University of California, Berkeley. He is the founder of the University's Peace and Conflict Studies Program, and currently teaches courses in nonviolence and meditation. Dr. Nagler is the author of *America Without Violence*, and, with Eknath Easwaran, an English edition of *The Upanishads*, as well as numerous articles on classics, myth, peace and mysticism.